JAZBUL MURID ILAL KHIDMATI ASHAYKHI

AN EXHORTATION TO THE MURID TO BE IN THE SERVICE OF THE SAINTS
<u>SHAYKH IBRAHIMA FAAL</u>

English Translation by Baay Demba Sow

CHAPTERS

INTRODUCTION

THE SHAYKH IBRAHIMA BEN MUHAMMAD BEN AHMAD

THE BASMALA

PRAISE TO ALLAH

THE FASTING

PRAYER: A COMMUNICATION WITH ALLAH

A BOOK THAT ADVISES RIGHTEOUSNESS

AN EXHORTATION TO THE MURID TO BE IN THE SERVICE OF THE SAINTS

AN EXHORTATION TO THE MURID

REVERENCE DUE TO THE PARENTS

OBLIGATION TOWARD A SAINT

THE CARDINAL VIRTUES OF THE MURID

BLOOD TIES

GLOSSARY

INTRODUCTION

Shaykh Ibrahima Faal (1855-1930) is the path that leads to Muridism. A life devoted to illuminating the way, Shaykh Ibrahima Faal was striking for his original practice, his total devotion and his allegiance to the Master.

At the core of Shaykh Ibrahima Faal is an in depth understanding of the Quran, Arabic and the teachings of the Prophet Muhammad (Peace be upon him).

This book was written between 1888 -1895 in Gandiol located in the region of St. Louis, Senegal. St. Louis was the French governmental capitol for the West Africa region, as well as a spiritual meeting point for the most prominent Islamic scholars.

Jazbul Murid was written as guidance to the Muslims but also as a response to the critics of Shaykh Ibrahima Faal's perceptions of Islam. Perceptions of Islam unknown by the Islamic scholars at that time.

Jazbul Murid can be considered a compass to show the path to the Muslims and to enlighten the skeptic about the meaning and the practice of Islam as conceived by Shaykh Ibrahima Faal who was determined to spread the message as far as possible.

While in Gandiol, two of the most respected Shaykhs took the extraordinary step of pledging allegiance to Shaykh Ibrahima Faal and becoming Murids. Those Shaykhs were Shaykh Mafalee Njang and Shaykh Ibrahima Sogg Taal.

However, the other two leading scholars, Shaykh Mayaree Jum and Shaykh Demba Yamb Joop, were very critical of Shaykh Ibrahima Faal for not performing the standard five daily prayers and not fasting during the month of Ramadan as recommended by Allah in Islam.

As a response to those scholars, Shaykh Ibrahima Faal took to the pen and wrote a book clarifying Shaykh Ahmadu Bamba's teachings. Thus demonstrating his perfect understanding of Islam. In this book, Shaykh Ibrahima Faal uses the Arabic language with dexterity, and shows his ability to use the divine text of the Quran to illustrate his message. This book is an exhortation to righteousness for all Muslims and to the Murids in particular.

> *"If this book is not from Allah, it is from those who advise righteousness".*
> <u>Shaykh Ibrahima Faal</u>

We did our best to translate this book written by Shaykh Ibrahima Faal to make it accessible to a wider audience and being faithful to his teachings, in the way we should interact with

people in general, Muslims, believers and our loved ones in particular:

> *"Open the gate of your house when they knock and welcome them in. If they get into discussion with you, then give them good advice, which will benefit every Muslim and believer. Giving good advice to people is much more valuable than a drop of blood shed for the cause of Islam".*
> <u>Shaykh Ibrahima Faal</u>

This publication has been made under the *Ndigal* (Recommendation) of Shaykh Rokhaya Faal, better known as Shaykh Ndigal Faal. This very *Ndigal* guided me through this work all the way.

May Allah grant him a long healthy life that he may continue to guide us for many years to follow the path of Shaykh Ibrahima Faal. May Allah also grant a long healthy life to the Murids and to the Muslims.

Our gratitude to Mamadu Mustafa Seck, who did not spare any effort during this work in the linguistic translation from the Arabic language into the Wolof language for more clarity, which allowed us to faithfully do our best to translate the original text accurately into English.

Our gratitude also goes to Oustaz Gora Jeetay, who rewrote the original text in Arabic using new technology such as the computer for better readability.

My gratitude to everyone who contributed in the final production, publication and distribution of this book.

Baay Demba Sow

THE SHAYKH IBRAHIMA BEN MUHAMMAD BEN AHMAD *

I seek refuge in Allah against Satan the Outcast. In the Name of Allah, The Compassionate, The Merciful. May peace and blessings be on our Prophet Muhammad. There is no might and force but in Allah, The Most High, The Almighty.

The Shaykh Ibrahima Ben Muhammad Ben Ahmad (May Allah guide him to achieve honorable actions). He is the servant who follows the Path renovated by his magnanimous master: Shaykh Ahmadu Bamba, who is his guide, his key, his enlightened judge, the righteous who guides the Murids through his wisdom.

The Shaykh Ibrahima Faal who clung onto the rope of his Shaykh Al Bakki*, who in his turn had clung onto the Tradition of the Prophet Al Makki*, the Erudite, the Ocean of Wisdom, the Shining Light, unique in his time and era.

Whoever follows him in the righteous path would be saved. Whoever walks away from him would be lost.

THE BASMALA*

The Shaykh Ibrahima Faal said concerning the Basmala that:

B of Bismi stands for the renunciation of sins
S of Bismi stands for the renunciation of the prohibited
M of Bismi stands as a motivation to follow the Prophet Muhammad (Peace be upon him).

Another interpretation would consider that:

B of Bismi stands for His Greatness
S of Bismi stands for His Splendor
M of Bismi stands for His Kingdom

While a third interpretation would consider that:

B of Bismi stands for the Mercy of Allah
S of Bismi stands for the Splendor of Allah
M of Bismi stands for His Sovereignty

Concerning the word Allah

A stands for the Oneness of Allah
L stands for His Mercy
L stands for His capacity to soften the heart of the believers
AH stands for His power to lead people in the paths of righteousness.

Allah is Merciful in this world and Especially Merciful in the Hereafter.

PRAISES TO ALLAH

The praises to Allah encompass four dimensions:

Praise from Allah toward Himself as mentioned in the verse:

All praise is due to Allah who created the heavens and the earth
*Surah 6 **Al An'am** 1*

Praise from Allah toward His servant as mentioned in the verse:

And to David We gave Salomon. An excellent servant. Indeed he was repeatedly turning back to Allah
*Surah 38 **Sad** 30*

Praise from the servants of Allah toward Allah as mentioned in this verse:

All praise is due to Allah, Lord of the worlds
*Surah 1 **Al Fatiha** 2*

And praise mutually given from the servants of Allah among themselves

These four dimensions belong ultimately to Allah who is the Sovereign of all His servants and of their actions.

FASTING

Fasting is only beneficial if it is aimed at celebrating the existence of Allah and if you preserve your four members from the temptations: The eyes, the heart, the ears and the mind. Do the same with all your members. Restrain yourself from eating and drinking.

Fasting belongs to Allah who takes care of its reward. It is only significant if you fast for the sake of Allah. Allah is both transcendent and immanent. How would you get close to Him if you do not make the journey by fasting?

Allah is immanent but He put a veil between Himself and some of his servants so they cannot see Him. According to some Sunni people, the veil may be lowered and the distance that separates them from Allah will progressively be shortened through fasting and then they will see Allah in Heaven.

PRAYER: A COMMUNICATION WITH ALLAH

Assert your intention to perform the prayer before you start your prayer or while you utter The Greatness of Allah: *Allahu Akbar* (Allah is Great) between the first letter **A** of the word *Allah* and the last letter **R** of the word *Akbar*.

The second call to prayer (*Iqamah*) is a Prophetic Tradition, while the sermon of the *Imam* on Friday is highly recommended to avert the Muslims from the many factors of this world that may lead them astray from the path of righteousness. Focus yourself in the prayer as if you were seeing Allah and communicating secretly with Him. Do not be present in the prayer with your body only, while your meditation is not with Allah and the Prophet.

Turn away from the illusions of this world and do not be preoccupied by them. Rather, meditate about the Hereafter and focus in your communication with Allah The Compassionate in order to obtain His Grace at the end of your prayer by consideration to the Prophet Muhammad (Peace be upon him).

Only Allah guides toward righteousness. It is He who guided Ibrahima Ben Muhammad Ben Ahmad Ben Habib Allah. May Allah make us benefit from His Blessings. May Allah grant us His Grace. May Allah reward our guide Shaykh Ahmadu Bamba and may He reward us by consideration to the Prophet Muhammad (Peace be upon him).

A BOOK THAT ADVISES RIGHTEOUSNESS

O You who meditate and have insight! Do not behave like those who disbelieve among the people of the Book and among the Polytheists, by opening my book, see the truth in it, yet reject it.

Those who disbelieve among the people of the Book and among the Polytheists, were not going to depart from their ways until there should come to them Clear Evidence.
<u>Surah 98 Al Bayyinah 1</u>

If this book is not from Allah, it is from those who advise righteousness.

If this book is not from Allah, it is an exhortation to the Murid to be in the service of the Saints.

O You who listen to me! Do not laugh at the Murids who do not desire anything else besides what pleases Allah The Most High and dedicate to the service of the Prophet Muhammad (Peace be upon him). Since the Prophet has passed away, the debt owed to him is to be given to his heirs.

I titled this book:

AN EXHORTATION TO THE MURID* TO BE IN THE SERVICE OF THE SAINTS

Do not laugh at the Murids since the gates of Allah are concealed in the hearts of the believers. If you desire the gate of compassion, knock at the hearts of the believers by pleasing them and take that which has been concealed in them. Make it an act of piety, an act of sincere devotion and put your hopes in Allah. Make Allah your companion because He is with you:

He is with you wherever you are.
And Allah is all Knowing and Seeing.
*Surah 57 **Al Hadid** 4*

Whatever you do, do it for the sake of Allah. Any action that has not been done for the sake of Allah shall be in vain.

Carry the power of Allah as your load knowing that He will not reward your deeds in this world, but that He will reward them in the Hereafter. Be in need of the divine light, which is everlasting. Any lights other than His shall perish. Be aware of His everlasting Reign. Any reign other than His shall end. Make the worship of Allah, your daily food. Any food other than the worship of Allah shall be lost in vain. Be drunk on fasting, praying, being generous in pious gift and being in the service of your Lord. Do not be intoxicated by the pleasures of women and the pursuit of power, that will make you lose your riches. Do not keep company in this world with those who have gone astray, for

they will never lead you to righteousness having themselves forgotten to practice it.

Do you order righteousness of the people and forget yourselves
<u>*Surah 2 **Al Baqarah** 44*</u>

AN EXHORTATION TO THE MURID

O Murid! How can you build while you yourself were built? Surrender yourself to me in order to attain felicity. Why would you carry a load while you yourself are carried as a load? Do not buckle under the weight of a heavy burden. Unload your burden. Do not be preoccupied by it. Believe in the remission of your sins from your Lord. Why would you trouble yourself with worries and dark thoughts while you are in the hands of a spiritual guide? Never take your hopes away from the veil of honor of your Lord and His decree. The keys to your hopes are in the hands of your spiritual guide. Lean back against his gate for the sake of Allah and aspire to his blessings. The gate of Allah has never been closed. Seek His Blessings with faith and piety as recommended by Allah:

If the people of the towns had but believed and feared Allah, We should indeed have opened out to them all kinds of blessings from heaven and earth
*<u>Surah 7 **Al Araf** 96</u>*

These blessings are the rain, the Angels, the Prophets and the Saints. Be satisfied with what we told you. All the gates of Allah are concealed in the hearts of the believers. If you are good to the believers, Allah will open the gates of mercy for you. If you trouble their hearts, you will endure the chastisement of Hell as mentioned by Allah:

Those who persecute the believers, men and women, and do not turn in repentance will have the chastisement of Hell
<u>Surah 85 **Al Buruj** 10</u>

You should devote yourself to work and give off your wealth to the Saints, to the needy, to the weak and to your loved ones. When your right hand gives, your left hand should not know it.

The prayer is required for both man and woman and the members of their bodies should decently be covered. When you perform the prayer, be mindful of death and let it be your provision for the Hereafter. Before you move to a new house make it a comfortable place to live in it. Desire what is in Allah and the Prophet Muhammad (Peace be upon him) and the reward will be in the Hereafter. Do not forget your final resting place otherwise you will find it all uncomfortable to dwell in it.

As a trader, if you want to make profit, you must quicken your steps on your way to the market. If you are slow, then leave early for the market. Be cautious not to make illicit profit as it spoils benefit. Be afraid of Hell and rather aspire to the Heavens since Allah said:

Each of those gardens brought forth its produce
<u>Surah 18 **Al Kahf** 33</u>

Do not be like a blacksmith who saves his pieces of iron in his toolbox, just to burn them away in the next fire.

REVERENCE DUE TO PARENTS

The reverence due to our parents is an obligation as mentioned in the Quran, approved by the prophetic tradition and unanimously agreed by the Doctors of Law.

Do as they tell you if it conforms to the divine recommendations, but do not do it, if it is forbidden or prohibited by Allah. Be gentle with them. Pray for them if they are both Muslims. Treat them well and be devoted to them like a servant would be toward his master. Allah advises us to respect them and pray for them:

And lower to them the wing of humility out of mercy and say: "My Lord have mercy upon them as they brought me up when I was small"
Surah 17 Al Isra 24

He also said:

And your Lord has decreed that you worship none except Him and to parents bestow good treatment. Whether one or both of them reach old age while with you, say not to them as much as "Uff" and do not repel them but speak to them a noble word
Surah 17 Al Isra 23

Talk to both of them with compassion and be good to them at all times and in all places. Do not treat them good in front of people and stop treating them so when you are left alone with them.

You will receive your inheritance from them if you are still alive after they pass away. They raised you to appreciate work and whoever teaches you to work for the sake of Allah did you a favor. Whoever teaches you to work for someone else besides Allah is ungrateful as mentioned in the Quran:

Indeed mankind to His Lord is ungrateful
And indeed he is to that a witness
And indeed his love of wealth is intense
*<u>Surah 100 **Al Adiyat** 6-7- 8</u>*

Allah acknowledges that parents may get weary. To always desire good for ones children is a challenge. Like a servant who controls his emotion to avoid punishment from his master, children should behave in such ways towards their parents. However, no parent wishes the inheritance of their own child due to the love they have for them. Instead, they wish for their children to receive their rightful inheritance in due time.

If you work for your parents and not for Allah because you desire riches from this world and a position in society, they may not complain about it. It may be, when you work for Allah they will complain. But remember that Allah is your Creator and that He is The One worthy of your actions. Allah said: "I am your Creator wherever you may be and I am The One worthy of your actions".

If Allah wants, He can kill you, your parents and children in an accident. If Allah wants, He can kill your parents and let you live. If Allah wants, He can kill you and let your parents live. Allah is The Provider:

And there is no creature on earth but that upon Allah is its provision and He knows its place of dwelling and place of storage. All is in clear register
*Surah 11 **Hud** 6*

These words are from an illuminated guide, the sincere Murid who had surpassed people of his generation, Ibrahima Ben Muhammad Ben Ahmad who also said:

"O Allah, The Assistant, we implore Your Guidance and Your Help, because there is no might besides You The Most-High, The Almighty. Glory to Allah who made the Prophets and His Chosen Ones, the vessels of His Divine Grace, who in their turn distribute it to the servants of Allah. Glory to Allah who made the Saints the Heirs of the Prophets".

O Servants of Allah! I recommend that you worship Allah in the way He prescribes it, which is to worship only Him, to fear Him and praise Him. He is the Giver of life and He is The Only One able to bring life again after death. I also recommend that you meditate about this world of illusion in which you live, since you were given a mind to think.

Allah is The One who knows everything about you while you do not have any knowledge of how He runs things. You do not know the beginning and neither do you know the end of what He decrees. Achieve good deeds in this world which has witnessed your birth and which will be your final resting place, where you will not be able to defend yourself from the punishment. Fear your Lord and worship only Him, because He acts without fear and nothing or nobody can upset Him, blame Him, forbid Him to do what He wants, compete with Him or oppose His Will. Remember the verse of the Quran, which says:

I have only created the Jinns and Men that they may serve Me
*Surah 51 **Ad-dariyat** 56*

O Men and Jinns! Worship Allah, fear Him and follow His Prophet, because those who follow Allah and His Prophet will be saved. However if you ignore the power of Allah, look at the example of the earth that Allah brought back to life after its destruction. How many seeds were wasted in the earth? To serve Allah is a beneficial trade with imminent profit. Wake up and meditate about it!

OBLIGATION TOWARD A SAINT

Approach the Saints with the intention to please Allah. However consider your dedication to them as a seed planted with the expectation to harvest the fruit of your labor. The intention is worth the action, as mentioned by the Prophet Muhammad (Peace be upon him). Remember the verse of the Quran:

So ask the people of the message if you do not know
*Surah 21 **Al Anbya** 7*

And this other one:

We have certainly seen the turning of your face toward the heaven
*Surah 2 **Al Baqarah** 144*

Someone who does not have water to perform his ablutions let him purify himself with clean earth:

If you find no water, then seek clean earth and wipe over your faces and your hands with it
*Surah 4 **An-nisa** 43*

Someone who finds himself in a place where he does not have a sense of direction or compass to show him the direction of the Kaaba* should assert his intention to turn to the Kaaba and perform his prayer. This is also similar with the Saints.

Therefore, if the Murids did not have the means of nearness to the Prophet Muhammad (Peace be upon him), they have to seek the means of nearness to the Saints as per the following verse:

O You who have believed! Fear Allah and seek the means of nearness to Him and strive in His cause that you may succeed
<u>Surah 5 **Al Maidah** 35</u>

Do not wait until the Day of Judgment to obey the Saints otherwise you will regret it. The opportunities to achieve good deeds will be gone. Those who have intentions to achieve good deeds, act on them now because intentions without actions are vain. It would be similar to a cloud without water. If you cannot afford to go to the Kaaba, then go the Mosque, with the intention to go to the Kaaba.

Shaykh Ibrahima Faal, May Allah be satisfied with him said:

The majority of people have turned their back on the Saints, thus turning their back on the Privileges of Allah. They would rather dedicate themselves to delights and vanities of this world in the pursuit of worldly pleasures. They are only worried to feed their stomach but they are not worried to feed the Scale of Justice (so no soul will be treated unjustly at all). A full belly will be of no use to them when the Angel will come to take their soul, neither on the day of the funeral nor on the day of resurrection. They were warned about it in the following verse from the Quran:

The Day whereon neither wealth nor sons will avail, but only he will prosper that brings to Allah a sound heart
<u>Surah 26 **Ash-Shuaraa** 88-89</u>

To the ones who cannot afford the pilgrimage to Mecca, let them keep their intention to go to Mecca, by attending the Mosque nearest to them. Those who do not have a camel let them be satisfied with their donkey.

Most people have turned their back on the Saints, one who has the capacity to illuminate a heart. They are only interested in women and power tempted by Satan. They rush in the acquisition of riches and key positions in society. They are not interested by the grace of Allah and His Prophet. They are satisfied with the company of their families, the counsels of their loved ones and the sermons from the Mosque. They were not concerned by the recommendations of the Saints. If sermons were enough, Allah would have not sent Prophets and Messengers as archetypes guides to mankind. He would have just given us the Quran and the Prophetic Tradition. But Allah blessed us with Saints who are gifted and invested with spiritual powers to guide those who read the Book, their families and the disciples who follow them. These Saints are the vessels of the Divine Grace. They have obtained the grace of Allah just like the Martyrs who died for the cause of Islam did and the Companions of the Prophet Muhammad (Peace be upon Him).

Most people have turned their back on the Saints, because they ignore that these very Saints could rescue them in their graves. They are only interested in women, worldly pleasures and food. They abandoned the rope of truth that leads to the Saints and prefer strong drinks, which will leave them with a hangover and food, which will turn to excrement. They do not pay attention to the Command of the Saints, nor do they devote themselves to their service. The Command of the Saints will last until the Day of Judgment. They do not listen to the recommendations of those who help them avoid the Punishment of Tomorrow. They prefer to listen to profane music, the sound of drums, the songs of mundane women and others who are lost, instead of listening to the virtuous and good mannered people who recommend righteousness and forbid evil. They are only interested by the profit generated from trade and the company of frivolous women; avoid the company of the good Muslims and the believers of a modest condition. They forget about their final resting place, being only concerned with their riches, which will be inheritance for their children, but will be of no use to them on the Day of Judgment.

Allah has bought from the believers their lives and their wealth and in return has promised that they shall have Paradise
*Surah 9 **Al Tawbah** 111*

According to the hadith* of the Prophet Muhammad (Peace be upon him), Allah said:

"O Servants of Allah! The Heaven is Mine. The wealth is Mine. Therefore buy my Heaven with your wealth"

O Brothers and Sisters in religion! Be mindful of your families, your loved ones and those who joined you along the way, in order to walk with you while you have little provision for the journey.

You were alone before you were born and you will be alone facing death without the company of your families and your loved ones.

Allah recommends to the men to educate their wives and family through exhortation and reasoning, to safeguard the blood ties and to obey the Divine Command. Just like you would do it for someone standing by the edge of a well and may fall in it, or for someone being on the brink of the fire pit and may get burned by it, educate your loved ones and your families not to fall into immorality and wrongdoings. Just like someone would run away when he sees a lion or a cheetah, or someone caught in his sleep by armed thieves would run away to stay alive, educate your loved ones and your families to run away from immorality and wrongdoings. Just like a soldier would fight his enemy with determination to kill him, educate your loved ones and your families to fight immorality and wrongdoings.

Protect your families from men with no moral values in the same manner you would protect your goat from hyenas or any other

dangerous animals. Keep your families away from places of distractions, where young men and women would gather all night long to have fun. Avoid futile conversation when in the Mosque, talking about issues concerning your loved ones, your families and debating about politics. According to the hadith of the Prophet Muhammad (Peace be upon him), in the Mosque only sermons and exhortation towards righteousness are allowed. Remember the following verse:

O You who believe! Save yourselves and your families from a Fire whose fuel is Men
*Surah 66 **At-Tahrim** 6*

Do not be impressed by those who are only interested by profit generated by trade, neither by the Bedouin Arabs, because what is in Allah is much better than distractions and commerce. Allah is The Best Provider.

The Bedouin Arabs are the worst in unbelief and hypocrisy
*Surah 9 **At-Tawbah** 97*

Avoid traders who are only interested by profit and the Bedouin Arabs, as you would avoid a cheetah or as you would avoid falling into a well or being burnt by fire or as you would avoid firearms. Make your worship to Allah and His Prophet a habit in the same manner you accustomed yourself to smoke tobacco, eat and drink.

Follow the recommendations of Allah, in the same manner you take care of your worldly affairs. Educate your families in the worship of Allah and His Prophet Muhammad (Peace be upon him), by performing the daily regular prayers, fasting during the month of Ramadan, spending wealth for charity after they have believed in Allah, the Judgment Day, the delights of Paradise and the afflictions of Hell. Strike a balance between right and left, between prescriptions and proscriptions. Do not lean towards the prescriptions and thus forget about the proscriptions and vice-versa. Save your families from the punishment of Allah. Educate them to follow the Prophet and strive with their persons and their wealth in the way of Allah. Do it without controversy or dispute, yet do it with a firm hand.

Stand for the people and mobilize them in the way to Allah. Pledge allegiance to a Saint that are heirs of the Prophet and surrender to him to be a Muslim, as mentioned in this verse of the Quran:

Indeed, Allah has chosen for you this religion, so do not die except while you are Muslims
*Surah 2 **Al Baqarah** 132*

Be ready to make the journey in order to search for a spiritual guide who has held onto an unbreakable rope that leads to the righteous path. If you do not leave your house to search for a Saint, you will leave it one day to go to your grave.

Meditate on this verse from the Quran:

There is no doubt guidance for those who fear Allah, who believe in the Unseen, are steadfast in prayer and spend out of what we have provided for them
Surah 2 Al Baqarah 2-3

It is your duty to follow the footsteps of the Saints who will intercede for the remission of your sins because you have not been blessed to witness the era of the Prophet Muhammad (Peace be upon him), as Allah speaks of hierarchy among mankind:

It is He who has made you successors upon the earth and has raised some of you above others in degrees of rank
Surah 6 Al An'am 165

We are only men like you, but Allah confers favor upon whom He wills of His servants
Surah 14 Ibrahim 11

If you do not leave your houses to follow the footsteps of the Saints, you will leave your houses to chase after women. If you do not leave your houses to follow the footsteps of the Saints, you will leave your houses to satisfy your worldly desires. If you do not leave your houses to follow the footsteps of the Saints, you will leave your houses to acquire riches. If you do not leave your houses to follow the footsteps of the Saints, you will leave

your houses to get food or to relieve yourself; your families will not prevent you from it.

Your families are more inclined to take you away from Allah than to get you close to Him. If you do not wish to meet with Allah, Allah may wish to meet with you. If your families and your loved ones keep you away from Allah, none of them will be able to either help you when death come or preserve you from the divine decree if you became blind, disabled or sick, even more so preserve you from the afflictions of Hell or to intercede in your favor. No one would be able to intercede for anyone that Day without the permission of Allah:

Who is it that can intercede with Him except by His permission?
*Surah 2 **Al Baqarah** 255*

If you chose to comfort yourself with the company of your families and your loved ones, you will one day find yourself alone with your sins and you will find nobody to intercede in your favor. People are more inclined to make you sin than they would recommend to you to worship Allah. They would rather keep you away from Allah instead of keeping you away from distractions of this world. They would rather encourage you to be stingy and save your wealth than be generous (with your wealth), which after your death will be inheritance for the widows and the orphans. If you follow such advice you will regret it in your grave because unfortunately such wealth will be of no rescue to you. People will never advise you to spend the

wealth earned from your commerce in the way of Allah. Not spending your wealth in the way of Allah will allow them instead to satisfy the needs of their families and their loved ones, thus offering a false sense of security and dreaming of an eternal life as if they were immortal. These very same families and loved ones complain and are devastated if you devote yourself to Allah and sacrifice your wealth for His Glory. But they do not complain or get devastated by the fate of the sinners and those who live in ostentation. They do not get upset if you boast, but if you humble yourself and shed tears for the sake of Allah, they will criticize you and avoid your company.

Detach yourself from the illusion of this world before you go to your grave. You will have all honors and the grace from Allah only if you humble yourself before Him. If you do not spend your wealth in the service of Allah for His sake only, you will find yourself alone in your grave. Everything that you spend in the way of Allah will be rewarded to you in the Hereafter. Therefore, do not use the favors of Allah and then worship someone else beside Him. Surrender to Allah and spend your wealth in the way of Allah. Spend your wealth on what you love the most and not what you love the less, which is the best way to attain Allah's good reward.

Never will you attain the good reward until you spend in the way of Allah from that which you love
*Surah 3 **Al Imran** 92*

Shaykh Mayaree Jum and Shaykh Demba Yamb Joop! Would you not give up your pride and worldly honors for the sake of Allah, so you have all the honors from Allah? No one can have all the honors from Allah unless he gives up all worldly honors for the sake of Allah. No one can have rest from Allah unless he gives up rest in this life for the sake of Allah. No one can have joy from Allah unless he gives up joy in this life for the sake of Allah. No one can have beauty from Allah unless he gives up beauty in this life for the sake of Allah. No one can have a family from Allah unless he gives up his family for the sake of Allah. No one can have children from Allah unless he gives up his children for the sake of Allah. No one can have riches from Allah unless he gives up his riches for the sake of Allah. No one can have dwellings from Allah unless he gives up his dwellings for the sake of Allah.

The virtuous and illuminated Shaykh is also the author of the following advice:

O Brothers and Sisters in religion! Make of the existence of Allah your own wealth, then you will be rich forever. Make the clothing of righteousness your garment, because that is the only garment that does not get worn out.

The clothing of righteousness, that is best
Surah 7 Al Araf 26

Let abstinence be your daily food and then you will be granted with divine light. Polish your heart through fasting while mentioning the divine Names of Allah (*Zhikr*) and be in contemplation *(Fikr)*. Make the Mosque and your garden places of worship. Replace your sleep by nocturne prayers like the virtuous ones. Remember these verses:

Only those believe in Our verses who, when they are reminded by them, fall down in prostration and exalt Allah with praise

They arise from their beds; they supplicate to their Lord in fear and aspiration
<u>Surah 32 **As-Sadjah** 15-16</u>

It is He who sends down rain from the sky; from it is drink and from it is foliage in which you pasture animals

He causes to grow for you thereby the crops, olives, palm trees, grapevines and from all the fruits. Indeed in that is a sign for a people who give thoughts
<u>Surah 16 **An-Nahl** 10-11</u>

Indeed, Man is only honored if he fears Allah. Therefore you can only honor a Man if he glorifies his Lord. To underestimate his blessings would be underestimating the very blessings of Allah.

The great and illuminated Shaykh Ibrahima Faal said:

Who spends time in the company of the virtuous ones will certainly be honored. Meditate about the people of the cave and their dog Qitmir.

They will say there were three, the fourth of them being their dog. And they will say there were five, the sixth of them being their dog
*Surah 18 **Al Kahf** 22*

Whoever sacrifices his houses and belongings for the sake of Allah will certainly be honored and whoever sacrifices the little he has will consequently be rewarded its equivalent.

O Brothers and Sisters in religion! Do you not know that millet and water is wealth for the needy as mentioned in this verse:

Righteousness is not that you turn your faces toward the east or the west, but true righteousness is in one who believe in Allah, the Last Day, the Angels, the Book, the Prophets and give wealth in spite of love for it, to relatives, orphans, the needy, the traveler, those who ask for help
*Surah 2 **Al Baqarah** 177*

Help people of modest condition, man and woman with your wealth. Would you compare the worldly chiefs, the Arabs and the traders to the servants of Allah?

O Muslims! Remember these verses:

Or do those who commit evils think We will make them like those who have believed and done righteous deeds
<u>Surah 45 **Al Jathiyah** 21</u>

The most noble of you in the sight of Allah is the most righteous of you
<u>Surah 49 **Al Hujurat** 13</u>

Would you be like the transgressors who were only interested in accumulating wealth, from a very young age to old age, who inherited that wealth from father to son? They would only be left with bitter regrets if a calamity takes their wealth away from them. They will have bitter regrets of their ignorance of Allah, The Sovereign, The Provider. Would you be like the worldly chiefs who are filled with greed, illicitly accumulating their wealth by betting on horses? Would you remain ignorant and in a state of loss and total confusion? Would you be like the traders who hoard money with no concern for their graves, do not perform the *Salat* and give neither the *Zakat* nor charity? Would you be like those who do not spend their wealth for a good cause and who do not meditate on the following verse where Allah mentions the reward promised to the believers?

Those who believe, do righteous deeds, establish Salat and give Zakat will have their reward with their Lord and there will be no fear concerning them, nor will they grieve
<u>Surah 2 **Al Baqarah** 277</u>

O You who meditate and have insight! Giving good advice is an obligation for every Muslim. Do not be like the profane musicians, the makers of praises who forget about their Lord Who created them and yet provides them with infinite blessings. Do not behave like those who are lost and who are concerned only by their worldly affairs and thus forget about the Day of Judgment. Devote through prayers. Spend your nights in devotion. Spend your wealth in the way of Allah, give charity to the poor, safeguard blood ties and be in the service of the Saints. The divine grace comes from Allah, His Prophet and the Muslims. Be constant and generous in giving advice to the people with gentleness after you have purified your body and polished your heart in order to attain perfection.

THE CARDINAL VIRTUES OF THE MURID

The cardinal virtues of the Murid are based upon six principles:

- Faith
- Optimism
- Fervor in devotion
- The sacrifice of his wealth in the way of Allah
- Humility
- Obedience to the command of the Saint

O Murid! If you respect these six principles, the heart of the people will naturally be drawn toward you. Never complain to your spiritual guide about your misfortunes. Do not desire anything, in a hidden or manifest manner, anything besides what your spiritual guide desires for you.

Devote yourself to the service of Allah to serve Him with:

- Your strength
- Your wealth
- Your mind

I have only created the Jinns and Men that they may serve Me
*Surah 51 **Ad-Dariyat 56***

O Muslims who sow your seed in the way of Allah! Do not mistake the barren land for the fertile land, the river for the sea,

the well for the spring. Those who trade their Hereafter for this life of illusion will only have regrets as Allah reminds us:

And verily the Hereafter is better for you than the present
<u>*Surah 93 **Ad-Duha** 4*</u>

Do not obstruct your gates from this life with your wealth while your gates to the Hereafter are widely opened. Do not marvel at the women of this world and forget the ones in Heaven. Do not waste your energy to anything else besides Allah. How could you be so obsessed with the women of this world and forget the chaste women of Heaven with their beautiful faces and their amazing fragrances, which surpass musk and grey amber? How could you forget about the women of Heaven with an exceptional beauty and enchanted perfumes? Women, who never get old, never get crippled; never get skin diseases or venereal diseases?

How would you make a journey with no provisions, no luggage, and no clean clothes? How could you forget about the Day of the Gathering?

How would you cultivate the land without a hoe, dig a well without a pickaxe, fetch water from the well without a container attached at the end of your rope? A plant can only grow if the seed has been previously sowed and then watered. Heaven can only be obtained by having a reverential fear in Allah and by achieving good deeds.

Wanting to cultivate the land without a hoe, dig a well without a pickaxe, fetch water from the well without a container attached at the end of your rope, see a plant grow without having previously sowed the seed and watered it is a total absurdity. Wanting to go to Heaven without a reverential fear in Allah and by not achieving good deeds is a total lack of respect toward Allah.

How could you expect to have breakfast tomorrow when you did not save anything from your dinner? How could you cook without fire and water? Whoever pretends he can do it, is a stupid fool.

How could you be grateful to the Prophet, his Companions, his Family and his descendants from the teachings of Allah without being grateful to your spiritual guide, your shepherd?

Meditate on the following verse:

On the same Day, the hypocrite men and the hypocrite women will say to those who believed: "Wait for us that we may acquire some of your light." It will be said: "Go back behind you and seek light."
<u>Surah 57 **Al Hadid** 13</u>

Those who turn their back on Allah after having received His grace will regret having traded the good for evil. Such will be the fate of those who turn their back on the Saints. Do not disregard

them, because if you were not blessed to be in the service of the Prophet, you have been now given the opportunity to be in the service of the Saints. Indeed, how would you reimburse a debt to the one who lent it to you if he dies before you honored your debt?

Allah has established the prayer only for the purpose that you may repent, humble yourself and get rid of your pride. He has established the fasting during the month of Ramadan only for the purpose that you may control the seven members of your body. Allah requests from you to sacrifice your wealth for His Glory and serve the Prophet, his Family, his Khalifs and his descendants.

However the worldly chiefs and the transgressors refuse to follow the prescriptions of the Prophet, the Khalifs and the Saints, and hold onto this world of illusion. The worldly chiefs and the transgressors are at the extreme opposite of the Prophet, the Khalifs and the Saints in the same way water is at the extreme opposite of fire. These are the enemies of the Prophet Muhammad (Peace be upon him), the Chosen One of Allah who embodies purity and who has neither hatred nor hostility towards the enemy.

O Brothers and Sisters in religion! Sacrifice your wealth in the way of Allah and devote yourself to Allah. Meditate on these parables: one well can produce an endless water source, one ewe can breed a flock, one seed of a palm tree can produce clusters of

dates, one erudite can train many erudite, one ember can provoke a great fire, a small quantity of seeds easily carried by one person can yield a great harvest difficult to carry by a group of people.

How would you like to reach Heaven without the guidance of a Prophet or a Saint? How would somebody who waited until the darkness of the night accompany someone who left early in the morning and even more so, if he had not followed his footsteps and directions? How would you make a journey with no provision and not being guided?

If you were not blessed to witness the era of the Prophet and you have not pledge allegiance to a Saint, know that if you miss to perform the prayer at dawn (*Fajr*), you can perform the prayer after the sunset (*Maghrib*). Know also that the sun rises in the east and sets in the west and in its journey, the sun remains in orbit by the Power of Allah for those who perform the *Salat*. If you do not have a camel to carry your load, then put it on the back of your donkey because Allah created all beasts of burden.

O People with insight! Do not be preoccupied by the reproaches of people. Rather think about your state before birth and your state after death because you were alone then and will be alone in death and nobody had and will have a say about it, for your only comfort was and is in Allah.

To conform to the recommendations of a Saint is not similar to conform to the hours of prayers. If the prayer were not performed on time, all the benefits that should have resulted from it would be lost. However the prayer will still have to be performed on a different time. When the sun disappears and the sky is completely dark, it becomes impossible to determine the time of prayer, which is regulated by the position of the sun; if the sun is the one we know, which appears among spheres and constellations.

However the sun of this world moves around the earth by the Command of Allah for those who obey the divine recommendations. This sun is the Saint. Just like stars surround the sun, the Murids surround the Saint. Be impressed by the Judge, the Holder of Decrees and Power who teaches you that. That Judge is Allah who said to Adam:

O Adam! Dwell thou and your wife in the Garden
*Surah 2 **Al Baqarah** 35*

Allah wanted to show Adam His blessings so he could appreciate them, could desire them fervently and then could worship Him with his offspring. However Adam and his wife were not dwelling in the Eternal Heaven but in one of the heavens because the vocation of Adam is to worship Allah.

I have only created the Jinns and Men that they may serve Me
*Surah 51 **Ad-Dariyat** 56*

Allah only created Awa the beautiful one from Adam in order to show him His Power and the power of attraction. From then on, Adam was to face the duty of action with the hope of a reward and the birth of his offspring who would assist him in his worship to Allah, which would not be an easy task. Allah, in warning Adam and Awa not to eat from the "forbidden fruit" wanted to dissociate those who were destined to Heaven from those who were destined to Hell.

The disciple can only benefit from the grace of Allah through his actions, his dedication, his total acceptance of Allah's decisions, his patience, his ability to wallow in his grief and by avoiding criticizing his spiritual guide.

The purity of the disciple should manifest in the way he takes care of his body and his external look. But it could be only useful if he does not forget to polish his heart and purify the members of his body. Do not forget to perform your ablutions and to put a veil on the private parts of your body.

The weapon of the Muslim is in the prayer, the repentance, the devotion in prayers at nights, the invocation of His Name fervently at all times, the control of all his the members, the consolidation of the blood ties which gives a long life. Be courteous with your loved ones. Do not be suspicious about them. Do not narrate everything you may see or hear. Be more observant of your own faults, of things that can destroy you, make you angry or unhappy. Speak less if you are wise and

avoid any action, which can destroy your soul. Be patient in improving people's behavior to attain perfection and never complain about your hardships undertaken in your quest for Allah.

Be ready to travel with your wealth and your persons to reach Allah. Maybe you will succeed through the deeds, which He prefers and then would you benefit of His Guidance in your efforts toward perfection. Surely serenity will come after times of hardships. Be in the service of the Prophet Muhammad (Peace be upon him), because it is a source of blessings which will be poured over you, will take away hardships and will soothe the pain in the same way clouds send down rain from the sky after a long drought and make the foliage all green again.

Indeed in that is a sign for a people who give thoughts.
*<u>Surah 16 **An Nahl** 10-11</u>*

BLOOD TIES

Strengthening and consolidating blood ties give longevity as mentioned by a hadith. The strengthening of blood ties prevents from diseases and therefore guarantees good health. It should not be taken lightly. If a Muslim and believer are in need, then help them out. Allah said:

The believers are but brothers, so make settlement between your brothers. And fear Allah that you may receive mercy
<u>Surah 49 **Al Hujurat** 10</u>

Strengthen and consolidate your relationships with your neighbors. Be patient with them. Avoid criticizing them, cursing them, speaking ill of them or embarrassing them. Do not be envious of their belongings. Repent and help them as much as you can. Help them to keep their environment clean or any other required tasks. Open the gate of your house when they knock and welcome them in. If they get into discussion with you, give them good advice, which will benefit every Muslim and believer. Giving good advice to people is much more valuable than a drop of blood shed for the cause of Islam. Do not be stingy towards the orphans and the poor. Guide them toward the path of righteousness and give them some consideration when they approach you. Be compassionate toward servants, women and children. Look after them and protect them. The Prophet Muhammad (Peace be upon him) said: "You are all shepherds and each shepherd will be responsible for its cattle".

O Murid! If the reality was unfolded to you, you will know that everything about this world is an illusion. Hunger and thirst wait for you at every step of your journey. Therefore, the best of provision is the reverential fear to Allah, The Almighty, the perfecting of your soul, the ignorance of people's reproaches and the courage to face hardships. Allah said:

Fighting has been enjoined to you while it is hateful to you. But perhaps you hate a thing and it is good for you and perhaps you love a thing and it is bad for you. And Allah knows, while you know not
Surah 2 *Al Baqarah 216*

Will you simply assume that Allah desires bad for you or will you find another excuse? Or will you trust another God besides Allah? Are you among those who prefer the company of those who love to keep an eye to their riches thus forgetting the soldiers of Allah? Will you chase them away from your homes? How can you run after thieves that have not entered your homes yet? Meanwhile how many sins did you commit? How can you manage wealth, which is not yet at your disposition? How can you mend what has not been broken yet? How can you destroy what has not been built yet? How can you look after something, which does not exist yet? How can you step out from somewhere if you have not been previously inside? How can you forbid the use of something, which does not exist yet? How can you prefer things from people and neglect things from Allah?

Those who clothe themselves with expensive coats should know that their clothes would not save their body, their bones, their veins and their skin from the hardships of time. They too, will see themselves buried in the earth. And if it was not for Allah, how could their bodies rise from death to be brought back to life? Where are their days of happiness? They became proof against them.

O Passengers of the boat! Do not overload your boat with stones. Do not make your goal the acquisition of riches and forget about your final destination. Never forget that what you have at your disposition has been once in the hand of someone else. Do not think that this life is eternal and forget that Judgment Day will come.

O You who have insight! Do not consider the earth in which you walk like a horse you would ride. A horse does not ride its rider; however whoever walks upon this earth will see himself one day buried six feet under.

If you climb a thorny tree, do not go too far in your ascension. Rather think about your way down.

Exalted is your Lord, the Lord of might above what they describe! And peace among the Messengers and praise to Allah Lord of the Worlds
*<u>Surah 37 **As Saffat** 180-182</u>*

GLOSSARY

Al Bakki: refers to Shaykh Ahmadu Bamba which family name was Mbacke (Bakki)

Al Makki: refers to the Prophet Muhammad (Peace be upon him) who was from Mecca (Makki)

Basmala: stands for Bismillah (In the Name of God)

Fajr prayer: one of the five daily prayers in Islam performed at dawn

Hadith: an authentic narration from the Prophet Muhammad (Peace be upon him)

Kaaba: the Kaaba is in Mecca. Its location determines the direction of prayer (*qiblah*) for all Muslim scattered around the world

Maghrib prayer: one of the five daily prayers in Islam performed just after sunset

Murid: someone who aspires to Allah

Salat: the standard five daily prayers in Islam

<u>Shaykh Ibrahima Ben Muhammad Ben Ahmad</u>: The full name of Shaykh Ibrahima Faal

<u>Zakat:</u> obligatory payment required by the Islamic law with wealth or property for charitable purposes once a year

كتاب
جذب المريد
إلى خدمة الأشياخ
[للشّيخ إبراهيم فال]

شارك في كتابته:

باي دِمبَ سو

محمّد المُصطفى سيك

غور جيت

أعوذ بالله من الشّيطان الرّجيم

بسم الله الرّحمان الرّحيم

وصلّى الله على سيّدنا محمّد وسلّم تسليما

لا حول ولا قوّة إلاّ بالله العليّ العظيم

قال الشيخُ الإمامُ السّالكُ نهجَ، المستمسك بحبلِ شيخه البكّيّ الّذي استمسك بسُنّة النّبيّ المكّيّ، العالِمُ العلاّمةُ، البحرُ الفهّامةُ، فريدُ دهره، ووحيدُ عصره، الّذي من اقتدى به فقد هدى، ومن أعرض عنه فقد ردى، ومن اتّبع سبيله فقد نجا، ومن رغب عنه فقد ردى، ذن اك إبراهيمُ بن محمّدِ بن أحمد، وفّقنا الله وإيّاه بسعي ما يُحمَد، فقال: وأمّا

الباء من البسملة فإشارة إلى ترك الذّنب، وأمّا السّين فإشارة لترك المكروه، وأمّا الميم فإشارة لطاعة رسول الله p، وقيل: الباء بهاء الله والسّين سناؤه والميم ملكه، وقيل: الباء بِرُّ الله والسّين سناء الله والميمُ ملك الله دائم الله، وألف الله إشارة إلى وحدانيّة الله، واللّام الأوّل إشارة إلى لطفه، واللّام الثاني لينه لقلوب العارفين، والهاء هدايته لهم، الرّحمان رحمان الدّنيا والرّحيم رحيم الآخرة، فالحمد أربعة: قديمٌ للقديم كـ**(الحمد لله الّذي خلق السماوات** شيخِه الهُمامِ، المفتوحُ الحَكَمُ

القائدُ المُريدُ بالحِكَمِ والأرض)[1]، أو قديمٌ للحادث ك(نعم العبد إنّه أوّاب)[2]، أو حادث للقديم كقولنا (الحمد لله ربّ العالمين)[3]، أو حادث لحادث كحمدنا لبعضنا، فكلٌّ لله لأنّه ربّ العباد وربّ أعمالهم.

[فصل في الصّوم]

والصّوم اعتقِدْ بأنّ نفعه مقيّدٌ بأن تقصد بنيّة وجود ربّنا مع صيْدِهِ بأربعةٍ: العينِ والقلبِ والأذن والعقلِ، فضابطْ أربعةً إليهم لأنّهم الحواسّ وبعدهم الحصنُ للجوارح دون أكلٍ

---

[1] سورة الأنعام، آية [1]
[2] سورة ص، آية [30] و آية [40]
[3] سورة الفاتحة، آية [2]

وشرب في كلّ ما دخلتنا عليهم، وأمّا الصّومُ لله الموافق للصّواب فأن تقصد به وجه الله تعالى فيه إشارة لأنّ الله البعيد القريب وأنت المطلوب، ومعلومٌ أنّ المدّة لا يفنى إلاّ بسفرٍ والله قريبٌ ولكن جعل حجابا بينه وبين بعض العباد حتّى لا تراه العيونُ إلاّ مُدوّره، فيها قولان، وقيل يرونه في الجنّة، وهذا القول فيه جماعة أهل السنّة، وكلّ من النّاس له دار والدّار إمّا جنّة أو نار، والمدّة الّتي بينهما بعيدة والسفر إليها الصّوم.

[فصل في الصّلاة]

والصّلاة فأقمْها بنيّةٍ قبل تكبيرةٍ وجب بقليل أو معه، وأدخلْها بين همزة "الله" والرّاء من الأكبر، والإقامة سنّة في الصّلاة والخطبة لأهل صلاة الجمعة مستحبّة للتسلّي الدّنيا وما فيها مع حضرة القلب والبدن كمن يرى ربّه ويناجيه، ولا تكن قائمَ الجسدِ والقلبُ يدورُ في غير الله تعالى ورسوله ﷺ، ودَعْ واخْذُلْ فُضول الدّنيا مع تفكُّر في أمور الدّنيا، بل تفكَّرْ في أمور الآخرة واصغَ بمناجاة الرّحمان راجياً نيل فضلِه بعدَ السّلام بجاه شيخه.

[فصلٌ «اللهُ الموفّقُ للصّواب»]

ولإبراهيم بن أحمد بن محمّد بن حبيب الله تعالى نفعنا الله تعالى بجاههم ورضي الله تعالى عنّا وعنهم بجاه سيّدنا محمّد صلّى الله تعالى عليه: أيّها الفاهم، لا تجعل هذا الكتاب من أهل الكتاب المنفكّين حتّى تأتيهم البيّنة، إن لم يكن من الله يكن ممّن يأمر بالمعروف، وإن لم يكن من الله يكن جاذبا للمريدين إلى الأشياخ، وأنت لم تسخر المريدين لأنّهم لم يريدواْ إلاّ وجهَ تعالى وخدمةَ رسوله صلّى الله تعالى عليه وسلّم الّذي مضى، لأنّ الدّين تُقضى بالورثة إن عدم فصدقه مباح.

سمَّيتُهُ »جذب المريد إلى خدمة الأشياخ« لم تسخر المريدين لأنّ باب الله مدخّر في قلوب المؤمنين، إذا أردتَ بابَ رحمةٍ قرعتَ قلوب المريدين وأخذتَ بما فيها، واجعلْ إيماناً وصدقاً عظيما واجعلْ عملا صالحاً ورجاء وحسنَ ظنٍّ مراقاً، فكنْ متأنّسا بالله تعالى وهو معك لقوله تعالى (وهو معكم أين ما كنتم والله بما تعملون بصير)[4] واجعل قوّته حِمْلَكَ لأنّه يدّخره ويُخرجه، فكُن ذا اشتغالٍ بنوره المخلَّد لأنّ كلّ ضياء يُطفئُ غير نوره، واجعلْ مُلكه مُلكا لأنّ كلّ مَلِكٍ سواه صعلوكٌ

---
[4] سورة الحديد، آية [3]

ومُلكه زائلٌ، واجعلْ غذاه غذاء لأنّ كلّ غذاء خلتْ وبقى، فاسكن بِسَكرات الصّوم والصّلاة مع البذل والخدمة للمولى، لا تُصبْك فيها سكرات النّساء والسّلطان فخذل مالك، ولا تلتفتْ في هذا الزّمان لأهل الفروع مع الفواحش يعني بذلك في هذا الزّمان لأنّهما لم يقضيا إلّا ما وجب ولم يجب شيئا لقوله تعالى (أتأمرون النّاس بالبرّ وتنسون أنفسكم)[5].

[فصل في أمر المريد]

أيّها المريدُ، كيف تبني وأنت بناء فاطلبْني أَتَجِدُ فسلِّم، كيف تحمل وأنت محمولٌ، لا تشغلْ

---
[5] سورة البقرة، آية [44]

حِلْمك فخفِّفْه، ولا تكن بنا أجلّ الضّلالة واستوت بحطّ ربّك حِملك راجيا حطّه، فكيف تُفكّر وأنت سلط، لا تُتْعبْ نفسك بالوسوسة والحيرة لأنّ مرادك لا تهتريه ستورُ ربّك وقدَرُه، وأمّا مفتاحك في مُرادك عند شيخك ولتجئْ ببابه لوجه الله لأنّ بابَه لم يكن مرتجاً، واطلبْ بركةً لقول الله عزّ وجلّ (لفتحنا عليهم بركاتٍ من السّماء والأرض[6]) بالمطر مثل الملائكة والأنبياء، فكفاك بهذا قولنا لأنّ بابَ الله مدخَّرٌ بقلوب المؤمنين، فإذا فرحتْ قلوبهم حرق قلبك إذا لقوله تعالى (إنّ

---
[6] سورة الأعراف، آية [97]

الّذين فتنواْ المؤمنين والمؤمنات ثمّ لمْ يتوبواْ فلهم عذاب جهنّم ولهم عذاب الحريق)[7] بذلك وجب الخدمةُ والبذل للشيخ مع إطعام المساكين والضّعفاء مع القرباء بعد ستر العورة واجبة في الصّلاة لكلّ حرّ وعبدٍ رجلا وامرأة من قميص وغيره، فكُنْ ذا رغبة في الموت وإصلاح دار الآخرة لأنّ كلّ بيتٍ وقربة لا بدّ له من إصلاحٍ قبل سكنى، وارغبْ بما عند الله ورسوله وذلك لا تراه إلاّ بعد الموت، ولا تنس دارك، إن نسيتَه وجدته رميماً عند دخولك فيها، وأمّا ربح عيرٍ في قدومه إن كنت

---
[7] سورة البروج. آية [10]

ذا تجارة فاحذرِ النّار لأنّها يفسدُ ربحا وترغب الجنّة لقوله تعالى (كلتا الجنّتين آتت أكلها⁸) ولا تكنْ مثل حدّادٍ لأنّه لم يُدَّخَر في صندوقه غيرُ حديد ومُقمحون يصلونها.

[فصل في برّ الوالدين وما وجب بين الوالدين وولده]

وأمّا برّ الوالدين واجبٌ بالكتاب والسنّة والإجماع، وهو أن تُعاشرهما بالمعروف ولا تعاشرهما في المُحرّم ولا المكروه، وارحمهما وادعُ لهما بالخير إنْ كانا مسلمين وأكرمْهما ما استطعتَ وكنْ لهما مثل عبدٍ لأنّ الله تعالى أمر

---

⁸ سورة الكهف، آية [33]

بالاحترام لهما ورحمة، وقال وهو أصدق القائلين (وقلْ ربّ ارحمهما كما ربّياني صغيرا[9]) ولقوله (وقضى ربّك ألّا تعبدواْ إلّا إيّاه وبالوالدين إحسانا إمّا يبلغنّ عندك الكبر أحدهما أو كلاهما فلا تقل لهما أفٍّ ولا تنهرهما وقل لهما قولا كريما[10]) وأحسِنْ إليهما في كلِّ حين وفي كلِّ موضعٍ ولا تُكرِمْهما بين النّاس وتركهما في خلاء لأنّك ترثهما إن كنتَ حيّا بعدهما، وربّاك لحبّ الخدمة، والخدمةُ لله تعالى ومن أخدمهما لله فقد أحسن، ومن أخدمهما لغيرٍ فقد كند، فقال

---

[9] سورة الإسراء، آية [24]
[10] سورة الإسراء، آية [23]

الله تعالى (إنَّ الإنسان لربِّه لكنود * وإنَّه على ذلك لشهيد * وإنَّه لحبِّ الخير لشديد)[11] ولم يورثوا أولادهم بالله كما أسلمتْ حشما لسيِّده، وكلّ ما تلد لامت ورثها ولدها، ولم يورثوا أولادهم لربِّهم لحبّ شهوات الولد إذا كنتَ تخديماً لوجه الله تعالى بكاء ويُسوّاهم والديك وإذا كنتَ تخديما لوالديك دون الله تبشّرا لحبّ نفع الدّنيا مع الدّرجات لأنفسهم، وإذا كنتَ تخديماً لوجه الله اشتكيا بذلك ولم يشتكيا في عدم خدمتك لله الّذي أحقّ أن يخدم لأجله لأنّه ربّ العباد وربّ أعمالهم

---

[11] سورة العاديات، آية [6]

لقوله تعالى (والله خلقكم وما تعملون)[12] إن شاء قتلهم وقتلك معهم وإن شاء قتلك عنهم، إن شاء قتلهم عنك واضمِنْ رزقاً لقوله تعالى (وما من دابّة في الأرض إلاّ على الله رزقها ويعلم مستقرّها ومستودعها كلّ في كتاب مبين)[13] هذا للشيخ الفاضل المريد الصّادق الفائق جِيلَهُ سيّدنا إبراهيم بن أحمد بن محمّد، فقال عونَك يا مُعينُ وبك نستعينُ ولا حولَ ولا قوّة إلاّ بالله العليّ العظيم، الحمد لله الّذي جعل الأنبياء والأولياء خزائن رحمته يقسمون رحمتَه بين العباد ثمّ جعل العلماء

---

[12] سورة الصّافّات، [97]
[13] سورة هود، آية [6]

ورثة الأنبياء. وبعد، فعليكم يا عباد الله بأن تعبدواْ الله كما أمركم به لأنّه سبحانه وتعالى ألاّ تعبدواْ إلاّ إيّاه، ثمّ عليكم بتقوى الله العظيم واذكرواْ المبدئ والمعيد وما معكم بلا علم ولا حسّ لأنّهم لو تعلمون شيئا في أوّل أمر وفي آخريّة وأخلصواْ بعادات الأرض الّتي فيها مسقط رؤوسهم وتصير موضع مُضطجعهم لا تدرون فيه ولا تقدرون عن دفع الأذى عنكم في صغيركم ولا في كبيركم خفّفواْ أحوال ربّكم ولا تخافواْ أحدا، هو الّذي يتصرّف ما يشاء ليس عنده من يلومه أو يمنعه عن شيء ولا منازع له ولا مدافع عمّا أراده واذكرواْ قوله

تعالى (وَما خلقتُ الجنَّ والإنسَ إلاّ ليعبدونِ)[14] أيا معشر الجنّ والإنس اعبدواْ الله واتّقوه وأطيعونِ ومن يُطع الله ورسوله فقد فاز فوزا عظيما، إذا جهلتم فرض الله فانظرواْ الأرض بعد موتها فأحياها الله تعالى، وكم تِلِفتْ نفقةٌ أي بذراً في الأرض إذاً وذا تجارة ورِبْحُه حاضر فانتبه وهكذا فرض الأشياخ تقصدواْ به وجه الله تعالى أيضا باتّحال تقصدون به الشيخ كما تقصدُ الأرض في الزّرع وترجو نيْلَ نفقةٍ في ذلك، وفي الحديث «نيّة المؤمن أبلغ من عمله إن نوى»

---

[14] سورة الذّاريات، آية [56]

في قوله تعالى (فاسألواْ أهل الذّكر إن كنتم لا تعلمون[15]) وقوله تعالى (قد نرى تقلّبَ وجهك في السّماء[16]) فمن لم يجد الماء تيمّم وعجز في استقبال الكعبة فقدر مع نيّة وكذلك بالأشياخ إذا لم يروْا خير الخلق قدّروه، لقوله تعالى (يا أيّها الّذين آمنواْ اتّقواْ الله وابتغواْ إليه الوسيلة وجاهدوا في سبيله لعلّكم تفلحون[17]) ولا تنتظروا إلى يوم القيامة وذلك ندامة عظيمةٌ لأنّ الأعمال مضى وبقى ندامة، ومن نوى فليعملْ و مانية بلا عمل كسحبٍ بلا

---

[15] سورة النّحل، آية [43] وسورة الأنبياء، آية [7]
[16] سورة البقرة، آية [144]
[17] سورة المائدة، آية [35]

مطر إذا لم تروا الكعبة فكافيكم المسجد مع التقدير.

[فصل: وله أيضا زاده الله فيضاً]

مرّوا ما في الأشياخ من منافع لهم عند الله وأسلموا لما في البساتين والأنعام لحبّ شهوات الدّنيا واشتغلوا البطون ولم تشتغلوا الميزان ولا ينفع ذلك عند نزوع الرّوح وعند الدّفن في القبر والحشر لقوله تعالى (يوم لا ينفع مالٌ ولا بنون إلاّ من أتى الله بقلبٍ سليمٍ)[18] مرّوا في الأشياخ من شفاء ونور القلب واشتغلوا ما في النسوان والسّلاطين صحبة إبليس وبادروا

---
[18] سورة الشعراء، آية [89]

إلى المال وبادروا ليكونوا ذا غنى والحُكّامُ في دنياهم ولم يطلبوا رضى الله ورسوله وصاروا فذّا لأنفسهم والعيال وإذا تكفى بقول جيرانهم والمسجد غير هدى الأشياخ، وذلك لو كان كافيا لم يُرسل الله رسلا أهل وحي والقرآن والحديث ويحصل وليّا ليكون الأولياء أهل الإلهامِ لأهلِ القراءة كما يهدون أهلهم ومن تبعهم من خادمٍ وغيره، وهم ذو مرضاتٍ كالشّهداء والصّحابة وأيضاً فالنّاس مرّوا بالأشياخ ولم يلتفتوا إليهم لجهلهم نفع الأشياخ في القبور ويسلّموا لما في النسوان والمزاح والطعام، وتركوا تمسُّكا بحبل الأشياخ

ويتّصلون إلى الماء الّذي يصير غوراً وإلى الطعام الّذي عاقبته غائطٌ وريحٌ دون أوامر الأشياخ مع خدمتهم لهم وذلك باقٍ غداً وهم لا يصغوْن للواعظين ولمن يزجرهم لخوف ضرّهم غداً نصيحةً لهم، ولكن يصغوْن صوت المزمار وضجيج الدّفوف وغناء النّسوان مع السّفهاء ولم يصغوْا للصّالحين ذي أدب يأمر بالمعروف وينهى عن المنكر بل يصغونَ ربحَ تجارةٍ وجهيلةَ النّساء ويحذرون جلساء المسلمين والفقراء كما يكدحون قبورهم إلى شواغل الدّنيا الّتي تصير ميراثاً لأولادهم الّذين لا ينفعونهم غداً شيئا لقوله تعالى (إنّ الله

اشترى من المؤمنين أنفسهم بأنّ لهم الجنّة)[19]، وفي الحديث صلّى الله عليه وسلّم «يا عبادي والمال مالي والجنّة جنّتي اشتروا المال بجنّتي»، أيّها الإخوان احذروا العيال والجيران أمّا الّذي أدرككَ في نهجة وما معك إلّا قليلا وهم يريدون الخلطة بصحبة وتلفوا زادك مع شرابك وأنت كنتَ فذًا قبل الوجود وبعدها غيبة بلا رجوعٍ ولا صحبة فأحرى بالعيال، إنّ الله تعالى أوحى بذين للبريّة بأن تعلّموا الزوجات والعيال بالوعظ والإنذار وحفظ الأمانة وامتثال الأمر مثل من قام في

---

[19] سورة التّوبة، آية [111]

حرف البير أو نار كما يكون أديبا، ففرّوا المعصية كمن يرى ليثا أو تنينا، واحذروا معكم كمن حضر بوجه جيش أو لصّ يقصدونك بلا سلاح، واحذروا العيال ونفسك بسمير الشباب عند العشاء وقبله ثمّ لنفسك في الحديث بالمسجد بلا إنذار ولا الوعظ إلاّ الفضول واحذروا العيال مجلس الرّجال بلا صداقٍ أو بعضٍ كما تحذر معزك من ضبُعٍ وسبع، واحذر جلوس مسجدٍ مع حديثه مع الجيران والسلطان لقوله تعالى (**يأيّها الذين آمنوا قوا أنفسكم وأهليكم نارا**)[20] ولا تلتفتْ

---

[20] سورة التّحريم، آية [6]

لذي تجارة ولا أعرابٍ لقوله تعالى (قل ما عند الله خير من اللّهو ومن التّجارة والله خير الرازقين[21]) وقوله تعالى (الأعراب أشدّ كفرا ونفاقا[22]) واحذر كما تحذر تنينا و بيرا ونارا ومِدفعا، واجعل عادتك طاعة ربّك ورسولك كما تجعل عادة فمك بشُرب الدّخان والأكل والشرب، واشتغلْ بأمر ربّك مثل ما تحتاج إليه في إصلاح الحال والسلامة، واجذب العيال إلى ربّهم وإلى رسوله ﷺ واجذبهم لله ورسوله وللصلاة والصوم والصدقة بعد الإيمان واليقين للوعد والوعيد، وكن قائما

---
[21] سورة الجمعة، آية [11]
[22] سورة التّوبة، آية [97]

بين يمين وشمالٍ في أمرٍ ونهيٍ لو أراد بهما الأذى لواحد لا تقبل ذلك، وأقدمهم إلى رسول الله في أموالهم وأنفسهم بلا تنازع أو تذبذبٍ، فكنْ شافعا للنّاس وأخرجهم لوجه الله ورسولهن وكن ذا تمسّك بشيخ وارث النبيّ ρ لقوله تعالى (إنّ الله اصطفى لكم الدّين فلا تموتنّ إلّا وأنتم مسلمون)[23] عليك بارتحال لوجه شيخ وذي تمسّك بحبل متين إلى صراط مستقيم، إن تغيبواْ عن داركم لله سوف تخرجون إلى قبوركم فانظرواْ قوله تعالى ([...] **هدى للمتّقين* الّذين يؤمنون بالغيب**

---

[23] سورة البقرة، [132]

ويقيمون الصّلاة وممّا رزقناهم ينفقون[24]) عليكم باقتداء الأشياخ إن لم يروْا لقوله تعالى (ورفعنا بعضهم فوق بعض[25]) وقوله (فضّلْنا بعضهم على بعض[26]) ليشفعكم من ذنوبكم وأنتم إذا لم تخرجواْ لله خرجتم للنّساء، إذا لم تخرجواْ للنساء خرجتم للعبٍ، إذا لم تخرجواْ لله خرجتم لمالٍ، إذا لم تخرجواْ لله خرجتم لجوعٍ وعريان وغائط وبول، ولا يعوقكم العيال لأنّهم استدراج ولا إدراجٌ، إذا لم تريدواْ للرّحمان وهو سوف يريد

---

[24] سورة البقرة، الآيتان [2] و[3]
[25] سورة الزّخرف، آية [32]
[26] سورة البقرة، آية [253]. وسورة الإسراء، آية [23]

إليكم إذا منعكم العيال والجيران عن الله فسوف يأتيكم ولم تجدوا عندكم من يُغيثكم بالموت وعمى والمرض والعرج وغير ذلك فأحرى من يغيثكم بالنّار وشدائدها ولا يشفعكم عنده أحدٌ إلاّ بإذنه، ثمّ إذا كنتم تؤنّسون العيال والجيران فسوف توحشون بذنوبكم ولم تروْا شافعاً لأنّ الناس يأمرونكم بالمعصية ولا يأمرونكم بطاعة الله، ويأمرونكم بترك ربّنا ولا يأمرونكم بترك اللّعب، ويأمرونكم بالبخل ولا يأمرونكم بنصيحة، يأمرونكم باحتكار المال إلى غدٍ إذا ماتوا ورث المال والزّوجات ويتيم الأولاد وتندمون ندامة

عظيمة في قبوركم ولم ينفعكُم ذلك، ولا يأمرونكم بإتلاف المال لله إذا كنتم في البيع والشراء كالتجارة في حال دنياهم العيال والجيران ذوو البشرى في ذلك الأمن خوف الهلاك وحبّ الشهوات بلا موت، وأمّا العيال والجيران فهم باكون إذا تخلّيتم لوجه الله الكريم، يبكون لعزّة الدنيا ويبكون للمعطين ولا يبكون للّاعبين والعاصين، إذا كنتُم ذوي تفخُّر وفخر لا يزجون بذلك وإذا كنتم ذا تضرُّع وبكاء لخشية الله جاذباً يلومونكم ويعدو إليكم إذا لم تخلواْ عزّتكم لوجه الله تخلّواْ إلى قبوركم فلا ينالون عزّة إلّا بعد ذلّة

لله، وكلّما دفعتُم قبل موتكم سوف تجدونه عند موتكم في القبور، ولا تأكلوا رزق الله ثمّ تعبدون غيره، أيا مَيارَ جم وِدنْب يَم فقوما وتخلّا عزّة لوجه الله فخذ الأعزّة لوجه الله فكُنْ عزّة بلا ذلّة لوجه الله فذلك استدراج تدركه، فلا يُنال عزّة إلّا بترك عزّة لله، ولا يُنال راحة عند الله إلّا بترك راحة لله، ولا يُنال شهواتٌ عند الله ربّنا إلّا بترك شهوات لله، فلا يُنالُ جَمالٌ عند الله إلّا بترك جمالٍ لله، فلا يُنالُ عيالٌ عند الله إلّا بترك عيالٍ لله، فلا يُنالُ ولدٌ عند الله إلّا بترك ولدٍ لله، فلا يُنالُ مالٌ عند الله إلّا بترك مالٍ لله، فلا يُنالُ دار

الآخرة عند الله إلاّ بترك دار الدّنيا لوجه الله الكريم.

[وله أيضا] للشيخ للفاضل الفهّامة سيّدنا إبراهيم بن أحمد بن محمّد رضي الله عنهم: يا أخي واجعل وجود الله مالاً لك بلا حشر المال لنفسك إذاً تنل غنى غير رميم، واجعل ستر ربّنا لباساً غير حرق لقوله تعالى (**ولباس التّقوى ذلك خير**)[27] واجعل طعامك وشرابك جوعا تنلْ شدّة الأنوار وأخلص القلب بالصّوم واجعلْ شواغله الذكرَ والفكرة فبدِّلْ بستانك وفراشك مقيل المسجد وقيام الليل إذا النّاس

---
[27] سورة الأعراف، آية [26]

قد رقدوا لقوله تعالى (تتجافى جنوبهم عن المضاجع[28]) لقوله تعالى ([...] زرعاً تأكل منه أنعامهم وأنفسهم أفلا يبصرون[29]) لأنّ عظمة العبد بوقار ربّه ولا تبجّلْ عبدا إلاّ أن تجد عظيما ربّه لم تصغر بشيء إلاّ بتصغير حامله لقول الشّاعر العلاّمة الفهّامة:

» ومنْ يُضَفْ لمنْ حوى تصدُّرا *** فـإنّـه لا بــدّ أن يُـصـدَّرا
فكلب أهل الكهف شاهدٌ لِما *** ذكرتُه عند جميع العُلمـا «

---
[28] سورة السّجدة، آية [16]
[29] سورة السّجدة، آية [27]

ومن توقّد نفقتَه سوف تبلغُ بمثله لم ينفعْ ذلك ألا يعلمُ أنّ الدّخن والماء طعام المساكين لقوله تعالى (ويطعمون الطعام على حبّه مسكينا ويتيما وأسيراً[30]) كما يعينون الفقراء بمالهم ويكرمون لنسائهم بها، أتجعلون السلطان والإعراب أندادا وذوي تجارة، أيّها المسلمون فانظروا قوله تعالى(أفمن كان مؤمنا كمن كان فاسقا لا يستوون[31]) وقوله تعالى (إنّ أكرمكم عند الله أتقاكم[32]) أم أنتم كنتم من أهل الشرك الّذين يأخذون المال من حين صغيرهم على كبيرهم بنتا ببنتٍ من ولدتهم وأنتم ذوو ندامة حين يأخذ الذئب

---

[30] سورة الإنسان، آية [8]
[31] سورة السّجدة، آية [18]
[32] سورة الحجرات، آية [13]

بالأموال أو ضبُعٍ أو كانت ميّتا أو سرق بها أو نَهِبَ بها ومضى وبشراك بلولا وليت أو لو كان كذا، وتندمون ندامة عظيمة لجهلكم الخالق الباسط الأرزاق أو كان لكم أندادا كالسلاطين في حشر الفرس طغيانا وجهلكم أنفسكم حيارا أو كنتم كأهل التّجارة بأموالهم وينسون قبورهم بربْحٍ ولم يُقيموا الصّلاة ولم يؤتوا الزّكاة ولم يؤدّوا صدقة لله ولا ينفقون أموالهم في سبيل الله ولم ينظروا قوله تعالى (الّذين يُقيمون الصّلاة ممّا رزقناهم يُنفقون[33]) ونصيحة المؤمنين واجبة لذوي العقول أو كنتم كذوي المزامير ومدّاحين عن خالقهم ورازقهم أو كنتم كأهل الدّفوف

---
[33] سورة الأنفال، آية [3]

واللّعب والمزح وتنسون يوم القيامة ألم تزجروا إلى الصّلاة وتسهرون اللّيالي مع بذل المال والصّدقة وصلة الرّحم وخدمة وليّ الله، وأمّا المرضات تدور من الله ورسوله مع المسلمين وكونوا شطين ناصحين النّاس مع رحمة بعد طهارة القلب والبدن يقصدون بذلك إصلاح حالٍ.

وأمّا **المريدون** فمرضاتهم بستّة أشياء: إيمانٌ، وحسن ظنّ، مع نشاط بخدمة، وبذل مع تذلّل، واتّباع أوامر شيخه، وتكن جاذب القلوب إليه، أيا مريدُ لا تكن ذا اشتكاءٍ عنده حوائجك الدّنيويّة ولا تُردْ إلاّ ما يُريدُ لك ظاهرا أو باطنا ولا يريد بقوله إلاّ بثلاثة قوّة

برزق أو عقل يرقّيه إلى الرّحمان وهو قوله تعالى (**وما خلقتُ الجنّ والإنس إلاّ ليعبدونِ**)[34] أيا زارعُ لم تلبسواْ العورة بسهل ولم تلبسواْ البحر بخوض ولا تجعلواْ العيون مثل الآبار، ومن يبع الآخرة بالدّنيا فسوف يندم لأنّ الله تعالى قال (**والآخرة خير وأبقى**)[35] ولا تقفلواْ المال بباب الدّنيا وبابُ الآخرة مفتوحٌ لكم في الدّنيا لا تصدّق نساء الدّنيا وتنسى نساء الجنّة ولا تفنواْ قوّتكم إلاّ بخدمة ربّكم، وكيف تطعمون النّساء ولم تختارواْ الأبكار الحسنات الوجوه اللّاتي رائحتهنّ أذفرُ من المسك والعنبر، وكلّهنّ لها متاع غير راثٍ

---

[34] سورة الذاريات، آية [56]
[35] سورة الأعلى، آية [17]

ولا خرقٍ وجمالهنّ يزدادُ كلّ يومٍ بلا هرمٍ وضنين ولا نقصان وبرص وجذام وداء فرج ذوات دفارٍ لوازم الذباب وكيف تريد بناحيةٍ ولا زاد معك أو متاعٍ صالح مع ثياب حِسانٍ وتنسى جماعة يوم القيامة كمن أراد أن يزرعٍ ولم يتزوّدْ بمنجل، أو أراد أن يحفر بئرا ولم يتزوّد بغسل، أو أراد أن ينال ماء البئر ولم يجدْ دلواً ولا رشاءً، وأمّا القصب لا يكبر إلاّ بالتماس الزّارع وماء المطر، وأمّا الجنّة فلا يُنالُ إلاّ بتقوى الله العظيم وعملٍ صالحٍ وأمّا غير ذلك فعدم أدبٍ عند ربّنا إذْ لا يُؤخذُ الحوتُ إلاّ في البحر مع صيدٍ وسِلكٍ لا ترجو غذاء ولم تدخّر دخنا بعد العشاء، كيف يُطبخ بلا ماء ونار، ومن أراد فسوف يكون

كحمارٍ براتحٍ وكيف تقضي من وكيلك من أُمّة محمّدٍ ρ وخليفته في ذرّيّته وذوي النّصوص عليهم السّلامان ِ من ربّهم ومن وكيلك بأحوالٍ لقوله تعالى ([...] **نقتبس من نوركم قيل ارجعواْ وراءكم**)[36] لأنّ كلّ من أنعم الله عليه مُنى فكفر فسوف يندم، يبدّل حسناتٍ سيّئات إذا رقبتَ أو عقلتَ فلا تغفل الأشياخ وكيف تقضي ديْنَ الضّامن إذا غاب الغريمُ أو عدم عند حلوله ولم يكن مُتلفه والقرآن لا قراءة وأكل مالهم القراءة وما أراد الله بالصّلاة إلاَّ أن يتوبواْ وإن تذلّلواْ دون الكبر، والأمانة في الصّوم أن تحفظواْ الجوارح السّبعة وتعطوا ما عندكم من رزقٍ وخدمةٍ لمحمّدٍ ρ ولذرّيّته

---

[36] سورة الحديد، آية [13]

أو خليفته أو ذوي النّصوص فأبوا عن ذلك فيأخذون بالفضول ومثل قبلة ذلك ولم يُرِدْ بسلطانٍ وكفّار ضدّهم مثلُ نارٍ وماء لا تقريب إذاً فثمَّ لمحمّد ρ عدوانا ليس له لأنّ جسمه طاهرٌ ليس فيه دنسٌ، هو المختار عليه السّلام، أيّها الإخوان انظروا كيف تجعلون بالبذل والخدمة فانظروا وتدبّروا لأنّ كلّ بئرٍ يُحفَر يصيرُ مورداً ويكونُ مُدّا واحداً ويصير ستّين صاعا أو أكثر، وشاةٌ واحدة يصير لها نسلا كثيرا، وحبّةُ نخل واحدةٌ يكون لها ثمرٌ كثيرٌ، وعالمٌ واحدٌ قد يكون له تلاميذُ كثيرةٌ، وجمرةٌ واحدةٌ قد تصير نارا كثيرا، والبذر يحمله واحدٌ إلى البستان خفيفا ويثقل جماعة إذا حُصِد، فليقسْ في ذلك ما لم يُقلْ وكيف يُريد بالآخرة

ولم يُزوِّدْ بنيّ أو شيخ في الأزمان، وأمّا الّذي غدا بكرة وأنت تروح عشيّة كيف تسير معه ولم تقتف بآثاره مع دلالة واضحة ولم يُعط بزادٍ ولم يقدْك قائدٌ وأنت إذا لم تجدْ رسولا في الدّنيا ولم تقبل بشيخ ومن معك وزادك أن تقضي صلاة الصّبح بعد المغرب، وأمّا الشمس فتطلع من المشرق وتمضي إلى المغرب وما جعل الله بينهما هدرا لأهل الصّلاة يكون بين الإبل والحمار حملا إن لم تجد إبلا فحمار يكفيك وكلّ بهيمة حاملة ذاتُ قُدوم من ربّها إليه، أيّها العاقل لا تبال بكلام الناس شكاية فانظر قبل مولدك وبعده ميتا وأنت كنت فذا ولم أحد شيئا وأنت تستأنس فيما بينك وبين ربك ولست مزامنة بشيخ كمراقبة وقت

الصلاة لأنّ الصلاة إذا فات المختار فات الفضلُ وبقى القضاء بأيّ وقت شئتَ والشمس إذا فات قرصها فات الوصال بها إذا كان شمس سماء تطلع من أفلاك وتسير في بروج السماء وشمس الأرض تطلع من الله وتسير فوق الأرض إلاّ بإذن الله وهو شيخ وكلّ شمس تحته أنجم وشمس الأرض أنجمها المريدون فأعجب كيف يكون الحاكم ذا قدرة وقوّة وتُفسَّر دائما والموجود بالكلام ولم يُرد الله تعالى لقوله لآدم (**اسكن أنت وزوجك الجنّة**[37]) إلّا أن يريه نعمته ليكون ذا رغبة مع تعظيم قبل أن يعبد هو وذريّتُه لأنّ جنّة الخلد لم يدخلها حقيقة ثم خرج من الجنة قبلها

---

[37] سورة البقرة، آية [35] وسورة الأعراف، آية [19]

(وما خلقتُ الجنَّ والإنس إلاّ ليعبدون)[38] وكذلك لم يرد الله بوجود حوّاء من ثقيل آدم إلاّ أن يُريه بثلاثة أشخاص عجبا لحوّاء جميلة وعظيمة خالط به رجاء خير وذا نشاط مع رغبة بعده مع نسل تُؤنّس ذا وحشة ويعينه في أمره لتجتهد في خدمة مولاه وكافٍ بالأحكام لأنّ الشخص ربّنا والحكم ثقيل وكاف مثل متاع وبمستقرّ لقوله تعالى (ومتاع إلى حين)[39] وأمّا الشجرة فلم يُرد الله به إلّا ليُفصّل بذات آدم بين أهل الجنّة وأهل النّار بقول الأرض لمّا جاءها إسرافيل ع وأراد أن يقبض منها واشتكى وقالت أنت تذهبها إلى ربّك وخلق بها

---

[38] سورة الذّاريات، [56]

[39] البقرة [36] و الأعراف [24] والأنبياء [111]

أهل الجنّة وأهل النّار قال لها إنّي أستحيي بك، والله تعالى حين أكل آدم الشجرة أراد أن يُفصّل الرّوح والبدن ثمَّ، وأمّا خزائن رحمة العبد في نشاطه وفعله ومواضع عقله، وأمّا الرضاء فبفعله والصّبر دون شكاية لما صُنع به ولا ينظر عيبا لسيّده وأمّا رغده في صيانته لم ينفع بطهارة البدن والثياب إذا نُسي صيانة القلب مع الجوارح، ولا تكن متأخّر الوضوء والغسل بعد استبراء العورة فالسلاح بالدّعاء والتوبة وسهر اللّيالي وابتهال في كلّ وقت إلى مولاك وندمٍ وضابط حواسّك مع صيده بعد تحصين الجوارح لوجه الله تعالى فبادرْ أيضا إلى صلة الرحم يزيد عمرك، وأحسنْ إلى جيرانك ما استطعتَ وأحسنْ ظنّك به ولا تُسئ

ظنّك به لأنّه العالِمُ بك ولا تنطق إلّا ما ترى أو تسمعُ وأنت فانظرْ نفسك وما يسوءه أو يغضبه أو يزيدُ غرامه فقلّلْ ذكر ذلك إنْ كنتَ ذا عقلٍ، فاحذرْ إن فعلتَ ما يسوءه فتجلدُ بإصلاح ما استطعتَ في كلّ حالٍ من أحوالِ النّاس فلا تُشِرْ إليه بسوء أبداً أو ارتحل بجميع شخصك ومالك لعلّك لقيتَه ممّا يُحبُّ طلوعَ إصْلاحٍ من الرّحمان لعلّه أن يُزحزحكَ غمام صهلوك الهدر مثل صحوٍ فاخدمْ لرسول الله ﷺ وسبب تبجيله تصبُّ وبله وموجه يبرّد ألماً وينفدُ تعبا كما يكون السحب هدرا للنّاس.

[فصل]

وأمّا صلة الرّحم تزيد في العمر كما في الحديث، وهي تُصحّ البدن إن كان فيه علّةٌ فَداؤه إن كان به سوء أو غرامٌ مثل خطوب وشرور لا تأخذوها سخريّة وهزؤًا إن عدم ما يصلح بهم ودام له إن كان ذا ضعفٍ فكنْ مُعينه بما يحتاج من أمر دنياه وآخِره لقوله تعالى (إنّما المؤمنون إخوة فأصلحوا بين أخويكم واتّقوا الله لعلّكم تُرحمون)[40] وأمّا الجيران فأصلحْ إليهم وارعَ حقوقهم واحمل وكن صائنًا أجسامهم بشتم وذمّ أو غيبة أو نميمة واحذرْ إذا خلطتَ عليهم ولا تحسدهم بما آتاهم الله من فضله واستغفر الله وكن

---
[40] سورة الحجرات، آية [10]

معينهم بحوائجهم ما أتوك للتّحدّث وانصح لهم ولجميع المؤمنين والمسلمين لأنّ النصيحة لأهل البرّ خير من الجهاد على الكفّار ولا تغلل يدك للمساكين واليتامى فأرشدْهم واحترمهم إن قصدوك فارفق الأمّة والعبد مثل الزوجات والأولاد، فأصلحْ أحوالهم وأرشدْهم فاحفظهم لقول النبيّ ﷺ «كلّكم راعٍ وكلّكم مسئول عن رعيّته»، أيّها المُريدُ للرّحمان ليتها كنتَ ذا فُتوحٍ لأنّ كلّ غذاء يفنى وبقى بالجوع والظمأ مع سفرٍ فالزّاد الأفضل تقوى الله العظيم وإصلاح الحال وعدم الالتفات للورى والوحشية وتهديدا ولا تخفْ يا سائرُ بالكلام وهمٍّ وظنّ تُهمةٍ ولا تلتفتْ على ما تكره نفسكَ لقوله تعالى (كُتب عليكم القتال وهو كُرهٌ لكم

وعسى أن تكرهواْ شيئا وهو خير لكم وعسى أن تحبّوا شيئا وهو شرّ لكم والله يعلم وأنتم لا تعلمون(41) أم أنتَ موقنٌ بما أراد الله به إنّه شرّ أم لك عذر معتذر به أم تُريدُ أن تُسلّمَ إلى غير الله أم تريدُ أن ترعى بمال ما أعدّ له مُجيئه وتنسى جنود ربّك سارعا أم تطرده إذا جاء وهو موردهم أم يئستَ لصوصاً قبل حُلوله كيف إصرارٌ بميلٍ ولم يلتفتْ إلى مجيئه أو كيف يُجبر شيئا قبل كسره أو كيف تهدم البناء قبل بنائه وترعى قبل أن تُرسِل ويدومَ ولم يُوجد أو كيف تختاف أحوال النّاس وأحوال الله حصنٌ لا يُرام رميما أو كيف تخرج ولم تدخلْ وكيف تمنعُ ولم تملك، وأمّا

---
[41] سورة البقرة، آية [216]

المدثّرون تعرفون للمسابق بأن يُضعفَ أنَ العظام والعروقَ مع اللّحم والجلد الّذي كان يلبسه الجسد كيف يئض بصروف الوجوه لو لا إصراف الله له يجد كيف من عجم إلى وجود، أين الأيّام واللّيالي والنّعمةُ الّتي كنتم تنعمونها فهما وثيقة، أيا راكب البحر لا تلبس سفينتك بالأحجار، لا تجعل تنفيسة عمدا أو تنسى المورد، لا تظنَّ بما ورد من غير يد حميله، أيّها العاقلُ لا تجعل الأرض مثل فرسٍ لا يركب راكبه وراكب الأرض ييئس إلاّ أن يركبه الأرض عند نزوله أيا رقيّ الشجرة الصّعب عليك أن لا تعلو معراجا ليسهلَ الأمرُ والسّلام.

سبحان ربّك ربّ العزّة عمّا يصفون وسلام على المرسلين
والحمد لله ربّ العالمين

ليعلم النّاظر أنّ الكاتب كتبه كما رآه

Printed in Great Britain
by Amazon